SACRED CE
AN[
DESERT LEGACY

All the best Sean,

Ian Prattis

2023

DR. IAN PRATTIS

Manor House

Library and Archives Canada
Cataloguing in Publication

Title: Sacred ceremony : and desert legacy / Dr. Ian
Prattis.
Names: Prattis, J. I., author.
Description: Poems and essays.
Identifiers: Canadiana 20230455611 |
ISBN 9781998938018 (hardcover) |
ISBN 9781998938001 (softcover)
Classification: LCC PS8631.R396 S33 2023 | DDC
C818/.6—dc23

Cover art: photo by Carolyn Hill

First Edition
Cover Design-layout / Interior- layout: Michael Davie
140 pages / approx. 20,000 words. All rights reserved.
Published 2023 / Copyright 2023
Manor House Publishing Inc.
452 Cottingham Crescent, Ancaster, ON, L9G 3V6
www.manor-house.biz   (905) 648-4797

This project has been made possible [in part] by the
Government of Canada. « *Ce projet a été rendu possible
[en partie] grâce au gouvernement du Canada.*

Funded by the Government of Canada
Financé par le gouvernement du Canada 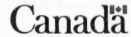 Canada

FOR CAROLYN HILL
And
AUTOBIOGRAPHY AT WORK

ACKNOWLEDGEMENTS

I am very grateful for the Testimonials in this new book. The views of each person provided trust in my work. It was a difficult book to write as the form travelled from the long way of my childhood to that of being an elder of 80 years. I think of my students at Carleton University in Ottawa and friends meditating at Pine Gate Sangha in my home. I dedicate this book to stand in their light moving forward.

This stretch has enabled me to write worthwhile books as *Redemption* got Gold at the 2015 Florida Book Award, *Trailing Sky Six Feathers* received the 2015 Quill Award. *Failsafe: Saving the Earth from Ourselves* in 2014 got the Silver for Environment. In 2019 *Our World is Burning* received Gold for eLit Excellence Awards.

I received the 2011 Ottawa Earth Day Environment Award and in 2018 the Yellow Lotus award from the Vesak Project for spiritual guidance and teaching dharma. Ottawa Independent Writers published some of my short stories in anthologies. I thank Bob Barclay and Mark Rossi for their belief in my work.

Thank you Suha Mardelli, Claudiu Murgan, Jana Begovic, Koozma Tarasoff, Krystina McGuire-Eggins, Lynn Adamson-Malelli, Carol Gravelle, Dawn James, Peggy Lehmann, Shobha Gallagher, Carolyn Hill, Germaine De Peralta, Judith Matheson, Iain Prattis, Nancy Brown.

My thanks also to publisher Michael Davie and Manor House for releasing my work to a world audience.

INTRODUCTION

Ian Prattis' new publication, **Sacred Ceremony and Desert Legacy** is another riveting medley of poetry and prose, autobiographical essays and a memoir of his mystical journey as a shaman and a Zen teacher. His gentle but powerful activism to save the Earth is the sacred glue fusing together all of the genres featured in this book.

Prattis uses the power of the word to remind us to open our hearts and our senses to the natural world, to hear the symphony in the whale song, and marvel at the flight of geese, or to "see spring blossoms cast a rainbow in summer rain."

Prattis' reflections on impermanence remind us that "our only possessions are the consequences of our actions", and that we should awaken from our apathy and slumber and show a renewed reverence toward nature becoming both leaders and followers of radical change.

His social commentary on wars and the destruction of our home Earth is couched in stirringly beautiful poetic language, which acts as a guiding light to beckon us toward a shift of consciousness.

- **Jana Begovic,** author, *Poisonous Whispers* and *Dragonfly Slayer*

TESTIMONIALS

"*Sacred Ceremony and Desert Legacy*" describes our world in words that are full of pragmatic hope. Ian's optimism that humanity can become symbiotic with Nature is contagious. From ashrams in India to barren deserts, Ian's words vacillate between wisdom of experiences and wisdom of the spirits to be mindful that not all the stakeholders of our fragile planet are human beings. Using enchanting imagery Ian reminds us that our future is of our creation but that also, we are not the only creators, and while we can get it wrong, there is always the opportunity—a floating bridge— to make things right. Thank you Ian."

- Suha Mardelli, Ottawa Independent Writers, Board Director

"With this, his twentieth book, Dr. Prattis takes the reader on an enchanting journey of discovery. *Sacred Ceremony and Desert Legacy* resembles a mosaic. But, instead of stones or tile, the mosaic is crafted with poems and prose, all interconnected by topics that hold a special place in the writer's heart. Dr. Prattis reflects on climate change, Indigenous wisdom and captivating spiritual journeys that he has experienced in his own life. As always with Dr. Prattis' work, the reader is left with more knowledge and wisdom. If you have enjoyed Dr. Prattis' previous works, this one will not disappoint."

- Krystina McGuire-Eggins, Therapist

This is a book about an open mind, an open heart, a troubled heart, sometimes enraged, sometimes tired and overwhelmed but always searching, always inquiring. It is a book about a man loving and living without fear, quietly listening to his own inner voice, a man who needs to whisper his words into the vastness of the universe, to plant a spark of light in the firmament to help guide lost souls home.
- Lynn Adamson-Malelli, Author, Artist

"Our determination to be peace and our courage to stand for it creates the force for peace and courage to stand for it. The author enters into deep listening, respectful communication, understanding to create bridges of understanding across the boundaries that separate us from one another and the Earth. Bravo Dr. Prattis!"
- Carol Gravelle, Writer

"Legacy" is the word I would use to comprise the essence of Dr. Prattis' latest book – *Sacred Ceremony and Desert Legacy*. He offers wisdom, experiences, assertiveness and activism of the highest quality. Beautifully captured in words that will last for future generations to enjoy, the desert is a living being, pulsing with energy, ceremony, and traditions." Re-reading the story of his prior books, I was filled with energy and awe for how much is involved in creating a Medicine Wheel. I would be humbled to receive such training if you ever think of leaving such legacy to others that you consider worthy."
- Claudiu Murgan, author-editor, *Love Letters to Water*

"When humanity becomes deeply rooted in remembering the impermanence of life, there's a chance our actions may evolve to honour the sacredness of all life and relationships with other humans, animals and nature. In *Sacred Ceremony and Desert Legacy*, Ian eloquently shows us that within each interaction and life experience, we can appreciate divinity and wonder, if we choose to be mindful and realize the interconnected of ALL that is...a weaving of hope, finding divinity in our life walk and mindfully tuning into the wisdom and messages from nature with humility, respect and reverence."
- Dawn James, Award-Winning author of *Unveiled: Autobiography of an Awakened One*

"In *Sacred Ceremony and Desert Legacy*, Ian completes his twentieth book, bringing together themes of his previous publications in compelling prose and eloquent verse. His autobiographical style encourages us to find our true nature by telling his own stories of struggles and human failings, his spiritual experiences and insights, and his lifelong devotion to planet earth. From the ashram in India to the wilderness of the Arizona desert, and the appearance of his wolf guardian who led him to his life partner, this book is engaging and inspiring, while also alerting us to the future we are creating through our choices."
- Peggy Lehmann, Author, Reiki Master

"A remarkable, insightful and engaging offering of literary essays and poetry advocating spiritualism and environmental protection and preservation.
- Michael B. Davie, author, *Great Advice*

TABLE OF CONTENTS

FOUR: PAINTING WITH WORDS

POEMS

FIVE: CARING FOR THE FUTURE

POEMS

Manor House Publishing Inc.
www.manor-house.biz
905-648-4797

ONE: GATHERING WISDOM

I presently live in Ottawa, Canada and encourage people to find their true nature, so that humanity and the planet may be renewed.

My poetry, memoirs, fiction, articles, blogs and podcasts appear in a wide range of venues. I bravely go into literary work, a stone tossed into the oceans of life.

However, it took a long time for me to step out on a journey of transformation.

As a young man I struggled with anger, violence, greed and being self-centered, though I was concerned about Mother Earth since childhood.

Indigenous First Nation elders taught me the ways and traditions to guide my way onwards. I knew that the achievements of these primal indigenous societies must become an integral part of our future human consciousness. They knew that the genocide they suffered was provided by the actions of clergy, colonialists and industrialists – stamped into their brains and hearts.

Now - I bluntly talk about humanity's future as precarious, brutal, and dark until we learn to save our climate, health and cultural emergencies.

As a university professor I had the experience of thousands of student dialogues and did my best to present history and context clearly, accurately and vividly.

The main theme was that there are two forks in the road. Which will we take? Dark, bone chilling and captivating, or inter-connectedness and interdependence of humans, community, and nature elements.

Relationships allow us to survive, thrive, heal and grow. The prevailing theme is survival and love in humanity and in nature - despite the challenges. Yet pathological consumption degrades our planet as industrial systems devour themselves. Are we at the end game without a philosophy for the future?

Our tomorrow will be shaped by the actions we take right now. There is still a short time to ground economy in ecological principles and the constraints of thermodynamic. We are in the midst of a health, medical, cultural and environmental crisis. The enemy now is us and our unsustainable way of living with others on our fragile planet.

What kind of future are we creating for our children? Do we teach them peace - acceptance, tolerance and self-worth? Or through neglect do we allow violence to flood their minds so they learn hatred and war? Even worse, do they live out our own personal wars expressed through our violent attitudes, speech and actions towards them?

I ask every adult, particularly men, to deal with their internal wars so that only the best in us is passed on to our children, not the worst in terms of violence. Our determination to be peace and our courage to stand for it creates the energy and power for change.

16

The first step is clear – we must deal with our internal wars, hatreds and fears. We must stop running and hiding behind addictions and busyness. We stop, look deeply into the eyes of our children and make a commitment to transform our internal demons by stepping on to the path of compassion, whatever our tradition.

We need community for this, to support us in sacred ceremony, meditation and creative spirituality so that we raise our consciousness and refine our speech, attitudes and actions.

We show our children the way to peace by learning to be peace. Let us be clear about the world we have created for our children. All violence is injustice and we have to teach our children the truth about war – greed, power, control. Not about winners and losers, but about the long-term suffering on both sides.

But the hatred grows, the suffering increases. What can we do as individuals to change this?

To prevent civil unrest and war, we must nurture non-violence within ourselves. We practice meditation and prayer in daily life to transform the poisons within ourselves and within our nation. Doing this in our family and in our community produces positive feedback loops throughout our society and government – which is ultimately accountable to each one of us.

We enter into true peace negotiations by learning the methods of deep listening, respectful communication, understanding and peace to create bridges of understanding across the cultural and religious boundaries that separate.

We create peace by knowing that compassion is the antidote to violence and hatred. This is the remedy for our troubled times.

Compassion, however, has to be generated in our heart by first of all taking care of our internal wars and violence. Then we are able to touch the depth of compassion, strength and clarity within us and take wise action. These actions are taken to the political and economic infrastructures that surround us.

As we injure Mother Earth, we injure ourselves. The rising sea levels and the burning wildfires produced by Global Warming will kill millions and displace millions more. We must change our ways and make peace with Mother Earth or we will not survive.

Our collective greed, mindless consumerism, industrial pollution and government irresponsibility must change.

We champion the cause of Mother Earth - of non-violent relationships in political and global affairs. This means our leaders have to be trained in the art of deep listening and stopping before contemplating violent action.

We must make it clear to our political and corporate leaders that business as usual is not an option.

As Ambassadors of Peace we must speak out to corporate and political leaders – not as individuals but as representatives of groups, coalitions and nations. As we go deeper spiritually, we realize everything interconnects.

We do not neglect the political and economic infrastructures that frame our lives. We hold them to account, we influence them with our clarity, wisdom and courage.

We consume carefully, rejecting the mindlessness of an uncaring consumer society. The future is now, for the actions we presently take are shaping the possibilities for future generations.

I listen to young people talk about hopelessness. They are concerned about the planet, job opportunities, growing hatred and wars. Prejudices, bullying, physical and sexual abuse are all affecting far too many people. Hope is not a feeling that magically makes us feel better and think that all will be well. Hope needs to be put into actions in order to transform.

We represent the diversity of the world – an example of what can be. This experience, however, evaporates into nothingness if we do not translate it into action. Begin the work on yourselves today, so that your attitudes, speech and actions become an example to your children, friends and communities. Take the practical steps to make peace with Mother Earth in terms of what you consume and support.

Then, represent your community, in coalition with other communities, to political and corporate leaders so they know the general public means business. But if we want them to change their ways – we first of all have to change our ways. Show clearly that we are choosing peace and harmony within ourselves, within our communities and with Mother Earth.

Taking action comes in many forms. Education is essential, meditation is necessary, some may protest, others may take action through artistic expressions – the possibilities are endless. I was an Anthropologist and educator at Carleton University.

I was a dharma teacher hosting a meditation community for 30 years. I was the founder of Friends for Peace and I write books.

My writing is that of a Poet, life as a Global Traveler, Guru in India, Zen teacher – enabling the spiritual warrior within to focus on planetary care, peace and social justice.

Since childhood I have scribbled poems and proses not found in my schools, universities and professorships. They seemed very closed aspects until I started to realize that Poetry provided the solitude of prose that enabled the greater note. In Sarawak, Borneo, India, Greece and around the world

I learned that dancing and singing of poetry was a basic signal of how to speak and write poems - at least for me! This, however, is the structure for this book, not knowing what will come out, yet I must try it.

20

Though it is not for me to write poems about Indigenous lore, the Residential Schools in Canada provided a genocide concocted by churches, governments, priests and nuns to eradicate their origins. I deeply cried and was also enraged at their cruelty, but realized that was not useful.

I created the Dr. Ian Prattis Scholarship for Indigenous, Black and Racialized students at Carleton University in Ottawa, Canada. I was a professor at Carleton University from 1970 – 2007 and present the scholarship to graduates that are diligent and intelligent.

With the discovery of the burials of Indigenous children all over Canada I urge readers to please donate to the scholarship to support Indigenous, Black and Racialized students to continue into our mutual future. Contact:

https://futurefunder.carleton.ca/giving-fund/dr-ian-prattis-scholarship-for-indigenous-black-and-racialized-students

I created the scholarship from the revenues of my books. The annual value is $2,000 and is awarded annually by the Dean of Graduate and Postdoctoral Affairs on the recommendation of the chair of the Department of Anthropology. This scholarship and my writing bring forward my responsibility of holding the pen as a posture to place words in a sequence that hopefully resonates in the reader's mind.

I have a sense of reciprocity about what I felt was necessary to heal the world from climate emergency and pandemic. The words play their part throughout as a sort of call and response meter that leans on kinship and community rather than corporate greed.

The poems and chapters in this book become as seeds in the mind of the reader, so my work cannot be buried or lost. The emphasis on Indigenous Wisdom pulls chapters together while being aware of how easy it is to fall into destruction.

1. Leaning Poses

Spectre with shadows

standing by knowing wisdom

from before, Coleridge and Darwin.

Echoes dawn sprawling open into a rugged desert,

stepping into screams

not expected under foot steps.

Cassiopeia – Andromeda's

stars draw our eyes

to find Kubla Khan's spasms

in strange poems

living breaths but no longer

in a land of warning vengeance.

Find kindness beyond the ghouls,

be reminded of mythic delight.

No longer seek bodies

stretch for high calla-lilies

beside the roses

in spiral depths name the stars,

leave all grief with the song of a harp.

2.   Resonation

The bridge lost the trains

where tracks buckled

and we met to share

false moments.

Such phrases creeped quietly

suspended by the dawn of logic.

Propriety categories await well known

slithering corridors.

Someone's eyes see mind

received by distractions

to plough the soil less damned.

Then the Muse

finds insightful pause

descending to hubris of mind,

resonating our being

as poetry surfaces with meaning

in the Cosmos.

3.   *War*

We circle the damage of war,

nerve center of our world.

Grimly aware that

transformation is changed.

We must rise and do it.

Taking ourselves then

others in swift urgency.

Otherwise we are marketable,

a glimmer rarely existing

where only Netflix clowns know.

If not, the memories

of war civilization

are no more than

Our Dead:

Yours

And

Mine

4.   **Indigenous Revival**

The Indigenous culture –

Ojibway, Cree, Haida

at the edge of the world – forgotten.

Yet they did not die.

Violence, neglect and hatred

could not destroy them.

Indigenous culture

lived against all odds.

Their hearts etched lakes, forests and mountains

Listening to a loon's call.

They know that forests stand in clouds.

The canopy of recurrent downpour

provides insights and instinct

that wipe the dark oblivion clear.

Old Indigenous culture keep alive

how to be human

and damn the genocide

placed upon them.

They know how to be human.

Old Indigenous culture

Ojibway, Cree, Haida.

They do that.

5.   *Mote in the Eye*

A Greek shepherd sprang into my mind,

as I watched pale images of rotund Zorbas

dance on the tavern floor in Athens.

Enthusiastic gyrates.

We spoke in many languages

to find the sentences, words, ideas exchanged

between the shepherd and I.

Dust spurned our toes

through olive growths by Epiros,

athwart Albania. Upon which we pissed

with alacrity to escape the attention

and bullets of border guards.

And I learned Greek from him

in the moment he received English from me.

Two youthful gods and friends.

Perhaps he remembers me.

TWO: FOUR PHASES RESTING

My 19th book, *FOUR PHASES: Lost, Impermanence, Bittersweet, Caring* , is about our broken world and Climate Emergency.

My books are not candidates for intellectual sophistry or theological nicety. It is the reader's inner experience of the words that is worthwhile. This leads to an escape that is strategic, to knowing and experiencing the energy of inner consciousness. When these dependencies are abandoned through trust in one's inner journey, celebrate what has always resided within.

Severe Climate Change is already upon us and needs swift action to give homo sapiens a chance of survival. However, the global pandemic and Russia's war devastating Ukraine affects the world from taking the route to a livable Earth.

The ultra-conservative Supreme Court of the USA in 2022 took a major step backward. It struck down the authority of the Environmental Protection Agency to tackle Climate Change – which is now a crisis they cannot change. This followed on their banning of abortion with respect to *Roe v. Wade*. Expect more mistakes to come forth from the Supreme Court.

Shobha Gallagher, a Freelance Writer and Film Maker, talks about this book:

"This is a deep journey through the heart of nature, her elements, the earth, ancient wisdom, the threads of the universe that are woven into our cells. Ian Prattis' new book explores planetary and environmental issues we have ignored and disconnected. It is incisive, a scalpel of poetic musings that probes the consequences of our actions towards nature, the planet, the responsibility of the legacy we are leaving behind for the next generations. This award-winning author has woven a montage of poignant essays, epiphanies, short pithy stories and our lost connection with family and generations. His voice breaches the surface to make us seriously ponder what we have ignored, shunned, or run away from.

I see his literary work as a shimmering river that flows into a collective soul-scape. We can hear and feel the scrunch of our feet as we walk through those forests, marvel at the fresh rhapsody and scent of spring shoots, the flaming russets and gold sheens of autumn. While creating that metaphorical clearing, the author also stokes that much needed long pause. Here we face our inner demons, anchor the wisdom of the Elders, and bring the urgent importance for the younger generation to understand "the meaning of rivers, forests and mountains."

I remember as a child how I blithely assumed that nature walked me when I cut school to roam the forest and rivers near my home. It brings back memories of

34

stretching time as I explored nature's domain. I still retain that childhood naivety about the web of life. I have always talked to birds, animals, trees, rocks and the planet. My speaking to nature provided me with an awesome, humbling sense of interconnectedness.

I have been an environmentalist all my life, long before I knew what the word meant. It emerged from an intrinsic love of nature and rapport with animals. I was often late for school, as the flowers and songbirds in the hedgerows captivated my attention, particularly in springtime, when creativity and new life exploded into being. I once attempted to explain my lateness in these terms to my schoolteacher. I was kept in at recess for my seemingly troublesome nature and made to write out 100 lines of "I will not be late for school."

I adorned my punishment schedule with drawings of birds and spring buds, and was then made to repeat the punishment. I did not understand this adult world, nor did I like it. Something in me persisted. I redid my lines, once again drawing birds on branches opening their beaks to sing joyously.

I was kept in at recess for an entire week for my stubbornness, yet refused to let go of my feelings for nature. Eventually the teacher gave up on punishing me for my drawings. I was eight years old, and that is when I learned to mistrust authority figures solely concerned with control and power.

As a child I had special relationships with wild animals, in particular with one otter and a family of hedgehogs that I kept under my bed. My parents were long suffering over the stray animals I brought home, but their patience was severely stretched over the hedgehogs. The hedgehogs had to be returned to the hedgerow when I became infested with their fleas, which I passed on to my immediate family, classmates, and also to a particular schoolteacher that I was delighted to so infest!

My passion for nature was solitary; it had no encouragement from any quarter because it needed none. I have subsequently made studies of wolf and dolphin behavior, and was "adopted" by a wolf. When I first met this creature, he was running free in the coastal mountains of British Columbia. He immediately claimed ownership — I was his! After showing me his mountain habitat and uncannily appearing every time I visited the Mt. Currie area, he chose to live with me in my hermitage in Gatineau Park Forest in Quebec. It was clear that he was a lone wolf and not part of a pack. It was in his mind to live with me in my forest home in Eastern Canada.

How did he know I lived in Gatineau Park Forest in Quebec? I gave him the highly original name of "Wolfie"!

The fascination with dolphins led to many adventures, studying and swimming with them in their oceanic habitat, ranging from the Outer Hebrides in the North Atlantic, to the Java Sea north of Bali, and in the Pacific Ocean off Maui and Vancouver Island. I was always exhilarated and totally humbled by their magnificent presence. For me nature was never to be conquered and mastered, it was simply to see my place in a vast, interconnected, and changing web of life. The poems in this chapter provide for humanity the vast aspect of being "Lost."

6.   ***Nature Ignored***

The treads of boots

leave prints in the snow,

banked softly in the quietness

of dark pines.

Looking down from high

the trees say very little.

Resting through winter,

memories in whispered moments

waiting for the Spring sap surge.

The jagged boulder

in the middle of the path,

another kill-site for Winter,

easily upends us,

bringing death everywhere

to the figment at the void.

The echo we cannot hear.

No memory weaves our mind,

static speaking over media chatter.

Too busy counting those lost in pandemic

while greenhouse gas infiltrates our lungs.

Thus, we are broken.

No voice beyond the senselessness

of this COVID death.

Just burning bodies in the frigid dark

ripping open without a chance,

while fireflies point stars

without knowing their names.

No longer do we speak of seasons

or notice the flight of geese.

There is only death

frozen in the forest.

Without sense of the loss

we blindly suffer

and decline to roam and rattle in lost realms.

Locked down sterile humans,

unable to procreate,

have now become our myth.

Everything else

stretches our lives, draws the veils

articulating crazy shifts.

Poetry takes us deeper if only we know how.

Trees, rivers, rocks, seas and mountains

survive in our absence.

Oceans are lost to our minds,

as we ignore

the language of whales calling.

- unable to hear their symphony,

or see spring blossoms cast a rainbow

in summer rain.

Boot prints in the snow

are all we leave behind.

THREE: IMPERMANENCE

The Buddha's Five Remembrances bring our attention to impermanence – on growing old, sick, dying, losing loved ones and realizing that our only possessions are the consequences of our actions.

The Buddha called on his followers to meditate daily – to live mindfully in each moment and to offer joy to loved ones. We seem to have forgotten the Buddha's guidance, as *Homo Sapiens* has radically compromised its existence on planet Earth.

From teachings on Impermanence, once we learn to accept the end of our civilization in its present form, we touch the truth of impermanence. This brings a certain peace and clarity to our minds and just perhaps we can implement structures and technology to save this planet of ours. Fear, despair and nihilism are useless. The means exist – the required mindful mentality is not there – yet.

We have a job to do in terms of cultivating a transformation in our consciousness to bring about a new way of living on planet earth.

Changing structures of greed and corporate dominance require first of all a change in consciousness. Mindfulness supports that outcome. Even deeper are the Buddha's teachings to spur a radical change.

Can we grasp the insight of extinction – of ourselves, our civilization – even of the planet. We have to find a way to adjust to our dramatically changed environmental circumstances. It all starts in the mind, which has to wake up to reality as it is.

Just listen......

Knowing I will get old, I breathe in.	Getting old
Knowing I cannot escape old age, I breathe out.	No escape
Knowing I will get sick, I breathe in.	Getting sick
Knowing I cannot escape sickness, I breathe out.	No escape
Knowing I will die, I breathe in.	Dying
Knowing I cannot escape death, I breathe out.	No escape

Knowing that one day I will
lose all I hold dear today,
I breathe in,

Losing what
I hold dear

Knowing I cannot escape
losing all I hold dear today,
I breathe out.

No escape

Knowing that my actions
are my only true belongings,
I breathe in.

Actions true
belongings

Knowing that I cannot escape
the consequences of my actions,
I breathe out.

No escape

Determined to live my days
mindfully in the present moment,
I breathe in.

Living mindfully

Experiencing the joy and the
benefit of living mindfully,
I breathe out.

Experiencing joy

Offering joy and love each
day to my loved ones,
I breathe in.   Offering love

Easing the pain and suffering of
My loved ones, I breathe out.   Easing suffering

The Buddha called on his monastics and followers
to do this meditation daily, so that their fears and
anxieties are welcomed into consciousness. In this way all
other fears may be transformed. The deep focus on the
realities of suffering in the past permits the meditator to
touch the Ultimate Dimension and take that energy back
into everyday life. Clear, concise and perfectly
compassionate.

About the Remembrances

I met a visiting Rishi in 1995 – a holy man from
India who recognized me and insisted I go to India for
spiritual training. I took leave from my Canadian
university and spent two years as a yogi, where the
spiritual treasures of India were opened to me.

I went there to teach and train in Siddha Samadhi
Yoga, a system of meditation for adults and children. It
was committed to global religious harmony and programs
to heal and transform deeply rooted schisms in Indian

society - through rural development, civic responsibility and anti-corruption programs.

There was also a marvelous outreach to introduce meditation into schools. colleges, universities, and factories.

I was privileged to experience so many treasures of India. While in India, in November and December of 1996, I became seriously ill. As I observed my body's systems crashing one by one, I knew there was a distinct possibility of death. I was surprised by my calm and lack of panic.

As December drew towards its close, I totally surrendered. I will always remember Saturday, December 21, 1996 as if it were yesterday.

On that day, I let go of all attachments to my body and surrendered to a sense of freedom never before experienced. I was living in a small ashram in the city of Mumbai – reserved for saints and holy men. I did not qualify for either category yet felt their grace at hand. I felt at one with all my spiritual ancestors, their wisdom, love, and gentleness as a tangible presence.

One humorous manifestation of that grace occurred one morning when I woke up and opened my eyes to greet one of my swami mentors. He smiled and helped me to sit up, then surprised me with his words: "We are all so happy Ian that you have decided to die with us in India, if indeed you are to die. And we will be most happy should you live."

To the best of my memory, I just smiled and said, "Me too!"

The swami made me some tea with herbs and beamed love and understanding to me before leaving. I felt very calm about the impermanence of my bodily existence. My heart opened wide. I thought about my many mistakes, and chose not to deny them or brush aside the bodily pain in this moment, for

I knew that the experiences of freedom were flooding through me. I felt very simple, that I was living properly, without panic. I did not fear death. This lack of fear opened a huge door to send love and joy to all. I felt my true self, peaceful, not pulled in any direction.

Despite all that was going on, I was solidly and timelessly present. I could freely share whatever gifts, skills and energies I had. I finally understood the significance of the Buddha's words about The Five Remembrances. To be with myself at this time, happy and content in the moment, was all I had. That was enough. As I practiced this meditation, I felt that each moment of life was absolutely precious and I was communicating this to all that I connected to.

Before I slept that night, one last meditation secured me in the refuge of all my spiritual ancestors. Although the focus was on the Buddha, I felt all my teachers and guides throughout lifetimes gathered together inside and around me, without boundaries, and they stayed while I slept. When I fell asleep, I was content and happy.

The next morning, to my surprise and joy, I woke up! Over the next six months, I slowly recovered my health.

My work in progress took me back to India six years later. My wife Carolyn and I embarked on a pilgrimage - In The Footsteps of The Buddha - through North India and Nepal in February 2003. We journeyed to Rajghir, Bodh Gaya, Varanasi, Sarnath, crossed into Nepal at Lumbini and then to Kushinagar, Vaishali and Sravasti.

I composed insight poems - a glimpse of experiences that are too immense to otherwise communicate. My wish was to record Living Dharma - people, life and experience in their vibrant mundanity. The Footsteps of the Buddha pilgrimage was full of wonder and miracles. It was a journey to the center of being so that everyday life becomes a pilgrimage.

Jana Begovic, Poet, Novelist, Editor of Ariel Chart Journal had this to say.

"Prattis nudges us towards a shift of consciousness in our relationship and each other. His disenchantment, with the state of affairs and the ever-increasing violence in the world and his rage with the discovery of torture and murder of children in residential schools, makes him take concrete action. He established a scholarship for Indigenous, Black and Racialized students at Carleton University in Ottawa, Canada.

Prattis succeeds in enlarging his reader's sense of sympathy and compassion for the planet. Prattis still writes with excited hope that we may wake up from our slumber of apathy and take action. He shakes us to the disturbing realities of climate change, injustices, cruelty and greed. His poetry and writings become a beacon lighting the path to an exploration of our capacities and potentials to bring more goodness to the world."

7.   Anger Boil

Touch the anger,

bring tears dripping down

your face and fingers.

Balance the scream

that permits your exit.

Step into the fire of nihilism.

The pallor of your body's dark history

wanders beside the tide.

Looking for the place

on the ruined planet

as jaguars growl at the boundary

intended to save you.

Who will rescue you?

What remains of our homesteads

boiled and burned in your anger?

Burn Out, Take Refuge

Over the years I have observed many young activist friends in the peace and environmental movements becoming overwhelmed and suffering from stress and burn out.

I firmly believe that activism without mindfulness practice will lead to burn out and disillusion of one form or another. I consider spirituality without an engaged expression to be equally unbalanced.

I encourage all of us embarking on this adventure in Peace and Planetary Care to root ourselves deeply in mindfulness practice on a daily basis. Touch the stillness of non-action first of all, so that our ensuing actions come from a place of effortless abundance and clarity. This is how we can take care of stress, burnout and disappointment. Guidance is essential.

Vietnamese Zen Master Thich Nhat Hanh, now deceased, specified very clearly how to reach out for help. He encouraged us in times of adversity, despair and burnout to take refuge in the community of spiritual practice.

Elder brothers and sisters in the community who are steady, patient and wise can help us step out of despair and anger by practicing meditation with us, returning us to mindfulness in order to take care of our distress. and take refuge in wise and steady friends.

We have to become good gardeners of the mind to do this. It takes skill, mindfulness and retraining to become a good organic gardener, so that the garbage in us is turned into rich compost. It also takes much understanding based on a non-dualistic view – accepting and recognizing just what is there in the mind. If our mind is dark with sorrow or anger, we recognize that this is just so.

With awareness we know how to practice walking meditation to take care of the mind-state recognized.

Without the darkness we would have no idea about the light dance of happiness. Instead of being overwhelmed, we use our skills of practice to recognize our mental states, nurture and transform them so there is no danger of being overwhelmed.

The mindfulness alternative of developing the necessary skills is a wise and therapeutic option. Activism is full of crises, curve balls and disasters. Mindfulness practice helps us.

PART FOUR: PAINTING WITH WORDS

8. *Autumn Seasons*

The waning sky casts hues and movement

To the stillness in the lake.

Promise of a more gentle time,

where winter's cruelty is cast aside

by buds of flowers

that insist on their dominion.

A clear diamond light of spring finds

the evening moon,

a delicate mistress, sees it all

anticipating the aging leaves.

Winter's swift warning

is quiet and mantled on trees

formerly vibrant with autumn's life.

In the rhythm of seasons,

the old ones

notice birds driven by winter's warning.

They fluff feathers and dance in the cold,

to tap on windows for the old man

to nail their feeder

reserved for their winter joy.

Summer's fruits given

to this stretch of nature's dominion.

The diamond light of spring

anticipates the aging leaves

that autumn gathers from summer's bounty.

Before the icy hand of winter

takes the land once again.

Nature's cycle undeterred

etches seeds of decay, silence and renewal.

An unseen hand speaks to us...

Listen to Her voice.

9. ***Ancient Tree in Winter***

Ancient Tree in Winter,

where did you come from?

Now trapped,

cleft by rocks at river's edge.

Water eddies carve your shape.

Are you hurt

exquisite sculpture of the forest?

Ice mires your branches,

snow creeps fingers across the river

as your body disappears under deep laden snow.

Decaying sculpture of existence.

Did you once stand tall and majestic

in a verdant Rideau River valley?

Host to birds, small animals,

insects and whispering breeze?

Were you alone on a high bluff,

shading thundering rapids

pulling you to their embrace?

What felled you,

so that you now lie here

trapped by rocks.

Exquisite beauty of my winter river walk.

Waiting for spring's flood

to set you free.

10. Dancing Trees in the Forest

Let me share it.

This symphony of autumn color,

cascading melody from a sky

pastel grey and fiery red.

Descant to tones of

a painted forest

cooled by lush evergreens.

Sensual beauty,

rhapsody of forest and sunset sky

fused a golden sheen,

caught in a still lake.

Waiting with patience

beyond time and space,

A pause to reflect this moment of weaving.

Silver birches silhouette the sky

gather in numbers,

elegantly, grace "en pointe."

They dance to gathering wind.

Murmur Creation's tones

in synchrony with stellar rhythms.

Their sound carries waves

to shoreline rocks.

Silver birches silhouette the sky.

dance for us.

11.   *Clouds and Eagles Dancing*

Clouds cascade from layered hills,

climb mountains

skirt offshore islands

with life shaping meanings.

Clouds,

universal alphabet of life and love.

Right here –

in these forests, lakes and mountains

in every human heart.

Clouds skirt layered hills,

mists and offshore islands,

touching Earth's syntax.

Gentle cascade

sunset fills the sky,

tracing cosmic runes

spelling Creation's name.

Insistent echoes pierce the sky

You are here

With us

We know you

From before.

Receive it

flight of Eagles.

Spiral mists descending,

treeline to shore,

now visible – then gone.

They weave a web.

Tapestry of land, lake and sky,

make Eagles of us all.

Mists of time

break and swirl, wings sweep

full circle. Eagle Creation

12. **Evening Poem**

Light of the sun climbs mountains,

rushing down the sacred canyon.

Islands of beauty,

shape Life's meanings.

As sunset fills the sky.

Tracing your name

to the rim of eternity.

Right now

in every heart.

Clouds shadow the canyon,

gentle drifting of evening.

All Our Relations Know.

13. Creation Calling

Resonance through time

unfolds the origin of Creation.

Stretching the songs of love

for the Universe to escape

and be different

to what it was.

Expanding this wish to the hearts

of oceans, trees, creatures and humans.

The drum of the Universe

clasped on my arm,

attuned to tectonic depths with ease.

I rest and learn

through skin, muscle, bone, guts

and the smallest atom –

that start light drives the world.

It begins with the smallest molecule

edging to Creation's direction,

through spectrums circling.

Compassion, clarity, seeking truth

bring life into splendour from darkness.

The Creation of the universe knows

authentic beings

without being a self.

Every molecule engages the Universal threads

in the warp of ruthless identity.

Floating free to the

largest constellation,

authentic rests

without ego, self or impression.

It infuses Love, Peace, Integrity.

Being is enough.

Casting realms of delight

to the passion of being.

Realms carried further

from dust sprinkled

through every warp.

That is where we belong.

14.   Dance of the Eyes

Enter the Muse – waiting

for cracks in facades crumble.

Grant life to dancing with the eyes.

Soft spoken adoration blows on dandelions,

parasols drifting to fertile ground.

Awakening pirouette turning en pointe,

while the waltz of happiness

leaves all sadness behind.

A funeral march to banish pain elsewhere,

before our eyes danced together.

Life lives in each glance,

cradled in the mosaic of

connecting where the universe begins and ends.

Delicate curves of elegant quadrilles

with the peace of loving serenade.

We dance with our eyes,

intensity of convulsive samba, cheek to cheek.

All in place, this dance of our eyes.

15. Opening in Mexico City

Trees shrivel smog shrouded in earthquake dust.

Urchins beg on the street,

"pesos por favor."

In Mexico City –

conquered land of conquering peoples

where Gods face all ways.

It was here I met you.

Forces unseen

that I had journeyed to encounter.

But not to this universe ...

Not with such violence.

I did not expect such a welcome,

such a death.

You met me.

Driving a javelin through my back

into my heart,

so that I was afraid of death.

Would there be courage in my dying?

Yet it passed

and as the fear was thrown away,

it dawned on my troubled mind

that this was the death of before.

Not an attack.

Just an opening.

This death in Mexico City

was your gift.

16. The Ascetic at Bodh Gaya

My wish is to record Living Dharma – people, life and experience in both their vibrance and mundanity.

I am not so interested in monuments and old bricks, being more in tune with the 14th Dalai Lama.

"This is my simple religion. There is no need for temples, no need for complicated philosophy. Our own brain, our own heart is our temple. The philosophy is loving kindness."

Water walking pilgrims

trace Gautama's searching footsteps.

Threads of centuries of quiet walking

Through sand, mud and fields

mere strands of Mother India.

Footsteps shared happily between pilgrims.

Deep silent journey

to emaciated Gautama's cave,

yet to receive succour

from Sujata's grace.

No shipwrecked words

followed his compass.

The Buddha's insight brought all pilgrims

to be seekers of Truth.

A morning meditation,

bamboo grove calling,

our hearts wide open.

Bodhicitta dancing with

graceful sweepers of fallen leaves,

behind a plough of words.

Heart wide open

with no horizon or meter.

Cascading into passages that hover,

tracing cosmic runes

at the edge of wisdom.

Words drift by in the morning mist.

A whisper of wind

finds every thought one breaths,

waiting wondrous so long

for cracks in facades order to crumble.

17. Return to Tulum

As tall reeds move with unison in a jungle pool,

selfie sticks clump in swarms

before the ancient monument of Tulum.

Their plastic smiles consume posterity

where I sat with reverence – many years past.

Vacant minds endure with pasted smiles.

I wonder if sacredness

penetrates unbridled progeny

of entitlement, noise and distraction?

Thirty years since I entered the walled city

of Tulum,

sequestered behind ropes and strict security.

The price of graffiti, looting and volley ball.

Even now the ancients could still be heard,

presence emerging with stillness and respect,

though silent to oiled sunbathers.

Whistle blowing security guards chase hooligans

from forbidden coastal bays and ceremonial pyres.

Marching them out of where they cannot be.

Years past I occupied those similar spaces,

but was bound with reverence.

No security guards to police my silent awe.

My whispered wish registers the Mayan radiance.

The Gods Face All Ways,

Beacon of ancient history.

Then later swarms appeared.

Legions carried the banner of language and culture.

Serious, bolder, organized, marching in order

like legionnaires in steps.

Tutored by multilingual guides, interpreters

and sages

carrying knowledge of Maya intelligence.

These legions dwarfed all selfies and hooligans.

The Gods Face Ways

Were recognized, not mocked.

Venus, the evening star of the Maya

appeared in the night sky,

as the walled city of Tulum emptied.

The Halach Uimic dynasty vibrated

through the five openings

of the walled city of Tulum,

into the ceremonial center,

Then East to the Castillo,

misnamed by Juan de Grijalva in 1518,

this majestic monument, a great palace

stood atop the cliff – crowned by a temple

complete with blood-stained sacrificial stone,

sloping steeply to the Caribbean Sea.

Before brazen tourism and tight security

I sat at this Upper Temple three decades past.

Alert to frightening corner-stones facing west,

emulated masks with mouths wide open,

teeth filed.

I stayed some distance from the sacrificial stone

placed on the cliff edge... and there it was.

A similar stone at the foot of the monument,

The mesmerizing energy from time before,

As I sat quietly upon it.

Before then, I could not put pen to paper.

Now – as you see – I can do so.

18.   *The Ascetic's Cave*

Gautama's searching footsteps

carry threads through sand, mud and

fields of quiet walking.

Footsteps shared with past pilgrims.

Then with awakening stirring

at Bodh Gaya,

Gautama became Buddha

when his ascetism was abandoned

for the Middle Way.

The Buddha's insight was granted to

all pilgrims,

seekers of the same Truth.

Heart wide open as the world awakes.

FIVE: CARING FOR THE FUTURE

Ancient Wisdom and Orkidstra take us forward.

During my career as an anthropologist, I was fortunate to encounter many First Nation story tellers across North America: Dene, Hopi, Ojibwa, Algonquin, Inuit – to mention a few. Their poetic recounting of myths and history had a deep impact on how I thought and wrote.

I would say that without poetry, cultures implode. Indigenous medicine people enhanced my process of remembering the power of the poetic voice. Through their mentoring,

I learned how to reconfigure my understanding of time, place and consciousness. I chose to listen to the sacred feminine voice of Earth Wisdom rather than the multitude of competing voices in my deep unconscious.

I made a radical turn in the 1980's to reconstruct anthropological methodology, as the poetic voice was always required for investigation of the cultural other.

I felt that the language of the anthropologist could not represent the raw experience of other cultures -

therefore poetry was philosophically essential to the work of anthropology.

I saw poetry as an uninterrupted process whereas field notes were not. I suggested to colleagues that the poetry of observation is what anthropologists are supposed to be doing.

Anthropologists who commit themselves to poetry in order to say something different about field experience are the tricksters and shamans of the discipline.

The radicalization of the discipline into a different kind of anthropology was required. I bring to Ancient Wisdom where an epic poem awaits the reader's attention. It was written when I accompanied two friends on the first leg of their cross Canada canoe expedition. I wanted to leave a document about Canada's wilderness for my grandchildren, so they could be inspired by Mother Earth.

When experience and inspiration sparked, I would shout out that I had to write. I would bring out the oil skin envelope stuffed with poems about the journey. I also wanted to weave in the Wisdom of the Elders, to speak about Canadian waterways from the reverence of First Nations, so that my grandchildren would understand the meaning of rivers, forests and mountains.

The words "without poetry, cultures implode" leaves the door open for our species and leaders to change. I choose to complete this story with a moment from the focus on Ancient Wisdom. In this poem I criticize human greed and its destructive impulses that result in pollution and contamination of the natural world.

I am nostalgic for the ancient ways of the people who had held Mother Earth in sacred regard, so I take readers into the heart of nature's Zen-like serenity.

In spite of being exposed to the merciless harshness of the elements, the poet – that is me - still smiles because I am a part of this world, just like a tree or a rock.

I see Ancient Wisdom as the tabernacle of our collective memory, and I harvest these ancient energies and weave them into my own history.

My poetry aims directly for the heart, speaking to the reader in clear and loud words, sometimes screaming the truth.

I take a small portion of the epic in order to talk about The Forest. The connection between humans and nature is illustrated with a solitary tree and a man. In each other's presence, their feelings of aloneness vanish.

19.   The Forest

Whisper of wind through pine needles.

Shimmering aspens and soft poplars of the forest.

Green – spring fresh green,

a relief to the year-round darkness of the spruce's

darker timbre and twin pronged sheaths.

The river denies our passage

so we walk through sheltered forests

rather than meet

our death by foolishness.

We wander and find herbs, trilliums white in dense

bush,

hiding among the wild strawberries

un-bodied with their

rich red summer promise.

Guardian trees, lichen laced,

protest the spring violets pushing upwards.

In the forest a great many entities

of the earth and sky speak of before

and what is to be.

Clearings sunk into the earth

await further visits.

In the center of one clearing

stood a single tall aspen - lonely.

Waiting for companionship,

fragile in its aloneness,

in her aloneness,

in our aloneness.

I stand within her circle

- this tree and I -

and for a brief moment,

neither were alone.

Orkidstra

Orkidstra is an Ottawa based development program that through music empowers kids ages 5 – 18, from under-served communities by teaching life skills – such as good teamwork, along with commitment, respect and pride in achievement.

Orkidstra started in Ottawa with 27 children in 2007 and now includes 700 children and youth, both in-school and after school from over 62 linguistic and cultural backgrounds. Children from lower-income families receive free instruments and music lessons. It is a social development program that fosters life skills.

Tina Fedeski, her husband Gary McMillen and Margaret Tobolowska founded Orkidstra after visiting Venezuela to research El Sistema, where it was established and then spread around the world.

El Sistema is a publicly financed, voluntary sector, music-education program founded in 1975 by Venezuelan educator and activist Jose Antonio Abreu.

Since 1975 "El Sistema" has used music education as a vehicle for social change. It cultivates an "affluence of spirit" which brings hope, joy and positive social impact to 400,000 children, their families and communities throughout the country.

This unprecedented success has inspired hundreds of similar programs, estimated at one million children in at least sixty countries around the world. The children become empowered and productive citizens.

El Sistema is an extra-ordinary cultural, educational, and social program that pursues the goals of social engagement and youth empowerment through ensemble music education. It has been growing for decades, where children living in impoverished circumstances learn to play and sing in orchestral and choral ensembles.

20. Weaving Autumn in the Canyon

Silver birches silhouette the sky,

gather in numbers,

elegantly, grace "en pointe."

Sway and breathe

bend and whisper in the canyon,

leaves shimmer

dancing to gathering wind.

Murmur Creation's tones

in synchrony with stellar rhythms.

Their sound carries waves

to shoreline rocks.

Silver birches silhouette the sky.

Light of Sun climbs the sacred canyon

rushing down islands

while shaping Life's meanings.

Sunset fills the sky,

tracing Creator's name

to the rim of eternity.

Right now in every heart,

clouds muster and shadow a

gentle cascade of evening.

This symphony of autumn color,

melody from a sky

pastel grey and fiery red.

Descant to tones

of a painted forest

cooled by lush evergreens.

Sensual beauty,

rhapsody of forest, canyon and sunset

fused as a golden sheen.

All caught in a still lake

waiting with patience,

beyond time and space

to reflect this moment of weaving.

SIX: DESERT LEGACY

The five prior chapters of this book provide a view of my autobiography in growing as a young man.

DESERT LEGACY takes it further into a realm of radical changing, mystic views and shamanic journeys. I begin with an amazing person. Dawson was a wisdom holder of many traditions – Ojibwa, Hopi, Lakota and the Native American Church. He did have a second name, but preferred Dawson. He was a legendary figure in Central Arizona and left a lasting impression on everyone he met.

I have encountered many people at conferences and talks all over North America and when it emerges that I have spent a considerable amount of time in Central Arizona desert country, I am always asked if I know a man named Dawson. He had met all kinds of people in his capacity as a guide and teacher. Yet his attention and presence never wavered in its intensity as he welcomed all into his orbit of wisdom and patience.

I first met him in 1987 on a day long ethno-botany field trip he offered in the Sonora desert region of Central Arizona. I was the only person to turn up, yet this did not deter him. He generously extended his knowledge of plants and hidden sources of water in the scrubland of the Sonora desert. His field trip skirted ancient medicine wheels created centuries ago. He talked about plant cycles within the teachings of the medicine wheel both for ceremony and healing. His mentorship has always meant a great deal to me, especially his instruction of how to build a medicine wheel.

Dawson was a slender yet muscular man in his sixties, though he seemed much older. His manner was slow and deliberate, gentle but firm though his light blue eyes carried a steely glint. He loved movies and would always sit in the çinema until the end of the credits, always the last person to leave. Eyes closed he made a point of downloading the full feeling of the film. It was the same with people, animals and the desert. He brought a sense of gentle intensity and intimacy to every relationship. The initial connection from that first field trip and movie experience warmed into a friendship. One evening in Sedona, two years after our initial meeting, I received a call from him. He asked if I would pick him up two hours before dawn the next morning.

"Wear hiking boots," he said.

I drove in the early morning dark to Cornville and found him waiting outside his house. I followed his directions to take various forestry roads leading to a reserve on the northern fringe of the Sonora desert. After parking we hiked for approximately thirty minutes into the desert through a scrubland trail. It was still dark when he gestured that we should stop. We shared a flask of coffee and the intense silence of the desert, interrupted only by the scurry of small wildlife. In the dark of morning just before dawn Dawson gestured for me to look in the direction of three large cacti directly in front of us. The sun rose and I could vaguely make out the flowers opening. Then Dawson pointed them out. They were absolutely stunning in their unreal beauty, ranging from yellow to dark violet. We sat there for over an hour, appreciating their beauty, as the morning sun rose.

"You had to see this before you travelled home to Canada," were his only spoken words. The morning heat was suddenly broken by a sudden hail storm. We put our packs over our heads and ran quickly to the shelter of the nearest rocky outcrop. The storm lasted only ten minutes although the stones were not small, making quite an impact on any unprotected area of the body. Dawson looked at me strangely.

"That sure is some kind of acknowledgement from the past, and it ain't for me. What have you been up to Mister Ian?" Dawson asked.

I just shrugged, as I had no intimations of cause. We walked in silence to where I had parked the car. The hailstones were not to be found beyond a hundred-yard perimeter of where we had been sitting.

"Beats the hell out of me, though I reckon you will have some building to do back in Canada," said Dawson cryptically, as he peered at me out of the corner of his eye. These were the last words I heard him speak. As was his custom we drove in silence. He got out of the car by his property, waved once and was gone.

On a later journey in 1992 to that region of Arizona, when enquiring about him, I discovered to my dismay that he had been killed in a car accident outside Phoenix. I was deeply saddened by this loss, thinking about all that he had so patiently taught me. I drove to where I had last walked with him, to pay my respects to this extraordinary spiritual teacher, remembering the way almost without thinking. It was not the time for the cacti to flower but I treasured once again the gift he had shown me. I wondered who he had passed on his vast knowledge to, then realized suddenly that he had passed on a great deal to me about medicine wheel lore and construction. Dawson was a spiritual guide and had taken me through many shamanic journeys. The hailstone storm was no longer a mystery to me, rather an early prompt. What I had received from him was put into place in the hermitage where I lived, in the Gatineau Forest in Quebec.

Over a period of five months in the spring and summer of 1994 I experienced very intensive shamanic journeys with an Algonquin shaman that I prepared for through fasting, meditation and sexual abstinence. On five separate journeys I met and dialogued with ancient shamans from the East, the South, the West, the North and finally to the ancient shaman of the Center. I figured at first that this was an experience with five facets of the same archetypal material from my deep unconscious, though there were major surprises I had not anticipated. Each shaman created distinctive unconscious energy within me, interconnected to the other four. In each journey I was always met by the same beautiful female figure, who then led me to the ancient shaman. Dawson had repeatedly told me that the feminine source would eventually emerge as a Muse for me, and there she was.

At my hermitage in the middle of Gatineau Park Forest in Quebec, I had a small circle of large stones in my front yard with beautiful ferns growing at the center. I had an overwhelming compulsion that summer of 1994 to build a medicine wheel with this circle of stones as the interior circle. I had been taught by Dawson the appropriate mind-state and procedure of respect to construct a medicine wheel. Dawson had instructed me intensely in Arizona about the central circle of the medicine wheel. It could only be truly experienced when connection to the sacred mystery was intact. The four cardinal directions, East, West, South and North, were the organizing axis for this ultimate fusion, represented by the ferns over which I took such care. It had sunk into my intellect but now reached my heart.

I constructed the medicine wheel with the assistance of two friends who shared my respect and training. We carried out the appropriate ritual, and worked with reverence on a very hot and humid summer's day. The silence that settled on all three of us spoke of something happening inside and around us while creating this architecture of incredible grace, power and beauty. The stones for the medicine wheel came from my garden and the surrounding forest, the hard granite of the Canadian Shield, part of the very ground where the medicine wheel was being built.

After filling the four quadrants of the medicine wheel with fresh garden soil, we contemplated what had been created. I realized its connection to my five shamanic journeys over the previous year. The cardinal points of the wheel and its center were a reflection of the five ancient shamans I had journeyed to meet and the ferns at the centre were an appropriate symbol for the feminine muse that delivered me. The medicine wheel was a symbolic map of my internal experience. I was re-inventing the wheel from my journeys to meet the five Ancient Shamans, yet also ensured that the beautiful ferns remained intact at the centre of the medicine wheel.

I started to smile at how this medicine lore and knowledge had gradually seeped into my consciousness from Dawson. His overarching influence had prepared me for the journeys to the five shamans. I could feel his intense blue eyes watching me at this moment and perhaps he permitted himself a smile too. It was his instructions I followed for my medicine wheel. He had known that I would eventually understand the wheel and the space at the center as the locale where I would seek counsel from the internal feminine - the beautiful ferns.

"There should be a Forestry Services road on the right-hand side about a mile ahead." I was juggling with a map and memories while providing driving directions for Carolyn. Our car slowly bumped along a rough road, deeply rutted by a flash flood from the previous week. We were just outside Sedona in Central Arizona and really needed an off-road vehicle instead of our rental car. I was looking for a sacred location I had visited before, near the Vultee Arch Trail – a natural rock arch separated from the canyon wall with a one hundred foot drop on either side. It had been created through time by cascading runoffs eroding the soft rock behind a harder rock ledge. It was named as Devil's Bridge by the cartographer who mapped it but a Cherokee guide told me the aboriginal name for the rock arch and stories of its sacredness. He asked me to refer to the location as Rainbow Bridge, for this brought into his mind the twin serpents of creation. This place of emergence was secluded and wonderful to him, and to me, once I became familiar with its mystical power. The medicine people migrating across the canyon floor had used it for millennia as a sacred ceremony location. For them it was a place of regeneration and connection to the spirit world - a bridge between earth and sky. Rainbow Bridge was where dimensions merged and changed. I was sure of this, though did not know how I knew it.\

The first time I travelled to this area of Arizona was in 1987 after an anthropology conference in Tuscon. The friends I was staying with urged me to pay a visit to the Sedona region, as they had a strong intuition that I would find a source of inspiration that I had lost. They were strangely prophetic with their insistence. I re-arranged travel plans and by good luck secured a ride from a conference delegate driving that way en route to Las Vegas. He dropped me off at Oak Creek Village and I found lodging at Quail Ridge Resort – taking a comfortable cabin for several weeks. I simply marvelled at the surrounding scenery. It felt like being in nature's cathedral, in the centre of a temple. The Red Rock country emanated a sense of familiarity that many people visiting for the first time feel intensely. I was no different. After settling into my simple yet comfortable cabin, on that first evening I took a flask of coffee, bread and cheese and sat at the foot of Eagle Rock – the aboriginal name for Bell Rock - not far from Quail Ridge.

I carefully looked over maps of the area to acquaint myself with the region's ambience. I saw that Oak Creek ran through the Red Rock country like a thread - drawing the canyons together. My exploration began with this Water element. This was one component of the Five Great Elements in Buddhist thought that I was familiar with – Earth, Water, Air, Fire and Space. I understood the sequence as the correspondence of all things to each other

101

driven by the feminine vessel of enlightenment. I have always thought of the present millennium as the century of the daughters. Not so much as a gender separate thing, but as attributes of a holistic, nurturing presence of mind. This is why I began my exploration of the region with Water. Oak Creek was fed by spring water from the sacred canyons and she carried their unique energies in one stream.

I began at Red Rock Crossing, fully aware that I was being guided by the feminine qualities of the region. But not aware of how deeply this river ran through me. I arrived at the crossing by taxi and asked the driver to return for me just before sunset. I stopped to look around at the awesome vista around me. This was where Oak Creek runs by the west side of Cathedral Rock – a majestic, soaring rock formation that defies imagination. I looked for the tall figures in the central towers, representing a Male and Female figure standing back-to-back. The myth was that they embodied the eternal values of harmony with all elements, earth and peoples. Black Elk's prophecy of the hoops of all nations interconnecting with harmony, no less.

Cathedral Rock's sandstone towers cast a shimmering reflection in the waters of the creek. Water, rock, sky, wind and fire – elements bound together in a seamless continuum. That is what I felt as I walked in the shallow waters with my hiking boots strung around my shoulders. From Buddha Beach – what an apt name - on a bend of the creek, I found a trail that led to the sandstone towers. I chose not to climb them. It was enough for me to stand in awe below them, with my feet firmly planted in the waters of Oak Creek. This day was about Water, not my ego.

I learned more about Oak Creek and its surroundings with several days of exploring Oak Creek Canyon to the north of Sedona. Always, I waded into the water so I could feel with my feet the pulse of the arteries of the entire area. I would lie down on larger, flat, dry rocks in midstream or perch atop rock rills and watch the water swirl around my feet, feeling a great sense of familiarity with this dramatic and melodious river. It was easy to explore the rim of Oak Creek Canyons, as the Schnebly Hill Formation was available by road from North Sedona, as it stretches into the highlands of the Colorado Plateau. I also took Brewer Road to the end and walked down the path leading to perhaps the most beautiful part of Oak Creek and listened deeply to the rhythm of this river.

During this visit I met Dawson - the wisdom holder. He chuckled at my apparent obsession with the Water element and clapped me on the back for addressing the feminine goddess of the region first of all. I shared his sense of the sacredness of this region and he tutored me over the next decade in the lore of medicine wheel ceremonies. He inducted me into the ceremonial cycle and shared some of his vast knowledge. Dawson said that I would learn to live the medicine wheel. The knowledge was already there – just needed to be tapped. With that introduction I readily embraced the medicine wheel's protocols of respect and reverence: always fasting before a medicine wheel ceremony, entering by the East, respecting the Creator, the Four Directions, Earth Mother and Father Sun. I was to do this in order to wake up. Not only myself but to soften the resistance in fellow beings. I had to promise Dawson to be open and vulnerable, so the power of the wheel could amplify my core energy.

Another privileged encounter was with Rion Hunter, a Cherokee guide. He was a magnificent looking man – tall, well-muscled and lithe with distinctive high cheekbones, his long black hair bound in a braid at the back. Rion took me, first of all, to Boynton Canyon. He explained that this was no ordinary trek. To the aboriginal people Boynton Canyon was the most sacred of canyons – to be treated with great respect. It was an enchanted place and a spiritual crossroads. Right at the entrance to Boynton Canyon stood an unusual rock formation – Kachina Woman. She cast the canyon into the goddess realm and stood on guard so all who were aware would know.

Rion offered prayers on behalf of both of us to the Earth Mother before we began the hike in. He related several stories from aboriginal lore about the canyon being the residence of the earth goddess. We hiked past "Enchantment" an upscale resort close to the entrance of the canyon. Rion approved of its location there, as he felt that the wealthy and powerful visitors would not be able to escape the power of the earth goddess. They would take it back into their corporate and political worlds for good measure. The majestic power of the canyon would work on them without their knowing exactly where their changed attitudes came from. I do so wish for this to be true.

Boynton is a box canyon – the way in is the way out. Only if the rim of the canyon is climbed could you come into it from adjacent canyons to the north. Rion led me to a small grove of ash trees off the narrow trail. The rock wall that the trees protected had a cleft in the shape of the female vulva. Rion related the legend that this was where the mountain gave birth to indigenous peoples. The entire canyon reverberated with this kind of intimacy, birthing and spiritual intent. After an hour's walk we started to climb a very sharp incline. A steep narrow trail led to a cave high up on the canyon wall, invisible to the human eye as shadows from jutting rock formations concealed it. This, according to Rion, was the cave of the mother. During a great flood, the mother goddess had tied herself to a log and floated up to the cave. At which point the flood receded leaving her in a new home. There she conceived a daughter from the rays of the sun thus beginning the indigenous peoples from godly sources. This was the story told by my Cherokee guide.

We reached the cave after an exhausting scramble. I noticed the remains of an adobe brick dwelling inside, from ancient times. Inside the cave there were rock shelves, once used for baskets, tools and weapons. In the back of the cave was a pool of fresh water accumulated from water seepage from the canyon's surface and through water condensation from morning dew. I also had a sense that the cave was once much bigger. It looked as though a rock fall had filled in portions of it. Rion concurred that this was possibly so. He took out a blanket from his pack and instructed me to wrap it round me and find a comfortable place in the cave to lie down.

Once I settled inside the ruins of the dwelling place, with my pack as a pillow – he conducted a ceremony of thanksgiving and remembering. He offered tobacco and burned some sage before playing his flute and chanting the sacred songs of the peoples who had used this cave for refuge – and though he did not know it, that included me in the realm of Eagle Speaker. I drifted off and slept very deeply with many visions from the past to keep me company. Rion had to gently shake me to wake me up. He grinned and said:

"I guess you were doing some heavy duty remembering to fall asleep while I roared the chants and played the flute. Time to eat – we'll make an offering to the goddess first – she gets hungry too."

I smiled at his humor and joined him at the lip of the cave. He made an offering of food to the earth goddess and we shared the rest. It was not for me to share the visions and feelings from the past, as I was stumbling into unfamiliar dimensions and territories, which I did not understand. So I ate and looked below me. The beauty of the canyon was breathtaking. We could see the trail far below from where we were sitting. No-one else had ventured up the steep incline, though we noticed the occasional hiker moving along the trail far below. We could see them but they could not see us. As we sat for a while at the edge of the cave, there was a sudden bullet like flash across the entrance.

"Was that a bullet shot?" I asked in surprise.

"No." Rion replied "That was a peregrine falcon at high speed. He must have spotted a quail or grouse below us." He chuckled at my astonishment that a bird could fly so fast. "It's also a good omen for your remembering. Believe me on this."

I did believe him and remembered from somewhere that such a falcon had made my visions come to life in a far distant life. Rion was quiet, seeing the remembering in my eyes, then pulled out his flute and played again. The haunting tones cascaded down the rock incline, merging with the trees, shrubs and rock below. He stopped and we enjoyed silence together. Then he said:

"We had better go now. Kachina Woman prefers that we are out of the canyon before sunset."

As we walked slowly down the steep incline and out by the canyon trail, there were tears streaming down my cheeks – I know not from where. Rion noticed the tears, but said nothing. From the trailhead we drove back to Oak Creek Village in silence. He gave me a big hug.

"Brother, we will go to the cave of the mother again in future years. Next I will take you to Rainbow Bridge – I can see that you are more than ready for that now."

Later that week Rion picked me up and we drove in by Dry Creek Road and found the forestry road leading to a trailhead. We walked in silence the two miles from the trailhead through oak and pine forest into the scrubland of cypress trees. The landscape felt somewhat eerie to me, as I carefully avoided the spines of the prickly pear cactus. I had brought tobacco and cedar with me from Canada. I had wondered why on earth I was taking these ceremonial items to a conference in Tuscon. Now I knew. They were not required in Tuscon, but right here at Rainbow Bridge. When I saw the natural rock arch, which was indistinguishable from the canyon rock at a distance, I

107

drew in a deep breath. It was stark and beautiful, separated yet joined to the canyon wall of rock. I was astonished by its presence. Instinctively I walked to the base of the archway and placed cedar on the rocks first, then tobacco as an offering to this magnificent natural edifice.

"Why did you do that?" asked Rion inquisitively.

"I just had to," I replied quickly, as though out of breath.

"Until I saw the archway I had forgotten that I had tobacco and cedar in my pack."

"That does not tell me why," Rion responded shrewdly, looking directly at me without smiling.

Right then, the words tumbled out of my mouth without thinking.

"Seeing the archway looming out from the canyon made it clear that I was to offer some sort of ceremonial recognition. Even walking in here with you, it felt very strange. As though the fabric of time and space was distorted – and I did wonder if this would be dangerous. The moment I could make out Rainbow Bridge and see it clearly – I knew why this is such a sacred place. I felt as though everything was converging here, readying me for a step beyond. Some how I know that Time and Space opens at the centre of the arch – that it provides a continuum with earth and sky, the past and future. For centuries this must have drawn the medicine people for sacred ceremonies. It was their place of connection with the spirit world."

The words stopped tumbling from my mouth and I felt a bit embarrassed at how I had poured everything out. Rion was silent for a long time, stirring the sandstone dust with the toe of his boot. Then he looked at me with his quizzical dark eyes that held a different recognition.

"I will show you the way up to the arch. You do not need me to understand dimensions opening, just needed me to show you the location. I'll be back for you before sunset."

After taking me up the canyon wall to the edge of the stone arch, Rion checked that I had sufficient water and then left. No-one else came near that day. I sat by the edge of the arch for some time. I was not afraid of it, just respectful. I listened and felt its rhythm and knew it was a matter of timing and invitation. When I felt that both of these were in place, I slowly walked to the centre of the arch, placing one foot carefully in front of the other. I sat down at the centre and went into very deep meditation with no sense of time or space.

I was there for a long time, feeling the splendour of the place while dimensions of time and space shifted and opened around me. I intuited that the dimensions were testing me, feeling me out to see if I could recognize what was going on. When I opened my eyes, the sun had started to set and there was Rion. He whistled with the high pitch of an eagle cry to get my attention. Smiling, he waved for me to move off the rock arch. The sun began to lower in the western sky, casting long shadows on the broad expanse between Rainbow Bridge and the sacred canyons to the west. I looked down on large ponderosas, Douglas firs and red barked manzanita trees. Across the Dry Creek canyon floor I could see the majestic rock formations outlined on the western horizon. Rion played his flute as we sat together at the edge of Rainbow Bridge. He put his flute down and said:

"You understand more than you say, so I will cut to the chase. Do you know why you have come here?"

I smiled, telling him of my friends in Tuscon who felt I would find what I had lost. He smiled gently and shook his head in slight exasperation:

"My friend – you do know there is more to it than that, though it will take a few visits for you to get it clear."

He picked up his flute and played until the sky turned a deep red over the western horizon. Then we sat in silence.

I knew these two destinations, Rainbow Bridge and Boynton Canyon were absolutely necessary for Carolyn and I during our 2007 sacred adventure. Once we had settled in at Quail Ridge after the drive from Phoenix, we went for a walk along the main street of Sedona. Noticing that there was a tour of the Medicine Wheels leaving in fifteen minutes, we immediately signed up. I thought this would be a wonderful introduction for Carolyn to the delights and wonder of the Red Rock country. We were the only two clients bumping around in the back of a small Jeep and our guide, who was very informative, took us to out of the way locations of the sacred wheels of life.

The tour was wonderful, particularly so when it coincided with one of those sunsets you can only see in Central Arizona. Yet, the main impact for Carolyn and I was a medicine wheel experience just prior to the sunset. Our guide stopped at an ancient medicine wheel that was off the tourist track. It received very few visitors yet welcomed us in an enchanting manner. There were bright yellow wild flowers lining the placement of stones – sufficient evidence that no-one had been there this season.

The guide – Sam – explained the signs to us. He was part Yaqui and part American with a university education and a deep knowledge of aboriginal traditions. For a large heavy man, he was very graceful and agile. His black hair was closely cropped and he carried his medicine pouch in a leather satchel strung round his back. Sam explained the protocols he followed and smudged us with some sage he burned. Carolyn and I meditated for a while, before walking in a clockwise direction three times round the wheel. We had removed our boots and socks so we could experience the earth with our bare feet. We were instructed by Sam to find the place on the wheel that drew us in. Carolyn stopped at the South cardinal point of the wheel. I carried on and stopped at the West cardinal point. The location for each of us was just where we felt compelled to stop.

Sam was a delightful mixture of aboriginal and new age. He had a pack of one hundred Native American Medicine cards and he asked me to shuffle the pack and cut it twice. Then he fanned the cards out, face down, and

111

asked me to select a card. The card was The Deer. He then read out the meaning of The Deer,

> *"Bringer of the message of a new paradigm resting on gentleness and compassion that serves the Earth Mother and penetrates all beings – no matter how wounded they may be. With great courage the Deer clears the path for others to reach their destiny with Spirit by taking away fear."*

It went on in that vein. Then Sam moved to Carolyn at the South cardinal point. She shuffled the deck and cut it twice. He fanned the pack out once more face down and invited Carolyn to select a card. He looked at it in total astonishment, then glanced over at me and back to Carolyn. "The Deer," he exclaimed. Then he read it out loud again very slowly to Carolyn.

> *"Bringer of the message of a new paradigm resting on gentleness and compassion that serves the Earth Mother and penetrates all beings – no matter how wounded they may be. With great courage the Deer clears the path for others to reach their destiny with Spirit by taking away fear."*

"Nothing like this has ever happened before. I've been using this pack for five years now. You both pulled the same card." He shook his head in disbelief before asking, "Do you know the significance of this?"

"Yes," I said. "It's not the same card. Carolyn is standing at the South cardinal point. I'm at the West cardinal point of the sacred wheel. We bring different qualities to bear on the significance of The Deer."

112

Sam's jaw dropped open in surprise at this insight. I continued,

"I'm at the West cardinal point and that brings New Beginnings, New Vision and a New Paradigm. Carolyn is at the South point – that's about grounding the Vision in everyday reality, supporting it and making it happen. The two locations work in combination to make it so."

"You know about this?"

I replied, "Somewhat. I had Dawson as a teacher over the ten-year period before he died. With what he taught me I also built a medicine wheel at my hermitage in the Gatineau Park Forest in Canada."

"Dawson, you knew Dawson? He was your teacher?" Sam exclaimed. "I would give a year's wages for that – he was a legend in these parts."

"He was more than a legend to me," I replied. "Dawson gave me a gift that I still offer thanks for."

We all sat down at the base of a large cottonwood tree, as Sam asked me to explain. I composed my thoughts before speaking.

"I was down in these parts a few years back and met up with Dawson for further training in medicine wheels. There was a sweat lodge at his place in Cottonwood that was quite unusual. He used a different set of rounds and introduced the third round as the round of the Red Wolf.

I think he got that from a Mongolian shaman who was passing through."

Sam slowly pulled in a deep breath, "I remember something about that."

"I had my own red wolf – a russet timber wolf - at home in Canada," I continued, "My friend Lisa was looking after him at my home in the forest while I was down here."

I described in some detail how I had come to know Wolfie and what an uncanny sense of connection this animal had with me.

"During the round of the Red Wolf with Dawson I suddenly felt Wolfie's presence in the sweat lodge, but did not pay it too much attention."

I went on to tell how Lisa had contacted me through Rion's phone number with the news that Wolfie had died. I was dismayed and devastated. When I phoned to Lisa in Canada, I learned that the timing of Wolfie's death in Canada coincided precisely with the timing of the Red Wolf round with Dawson. After putting the phone down I knew I had to talk to Dawson. I put on my jacket and picked up the car keys and opened my cabin door. Dawson was just pulling up in his truck. He got out and strode over to me. In characteristic manner Dawson came straight to the point.

"Something strange was going on with you during the Red Wolf round in the sweat lodge."

I gasped and burst into tears, as Dawson put his powerful arms around me for comfort. Through my sobs I told him what had happened. Dawson was quite gentle but firm.

"We need to do a journey for this one Ian. Before coming here I took the precaution of asking my fire keeper to prepare the grandfather stones for a sweat lodge at my place. That's where you can journey and find out just what happened. And don't try to tell me that you don't journey, for I know different. Now get in my truck."

On the drive to his home near Cottonwood, I related to Dawson the story of Wolfie. By the time we arrived at his sweat lodge I was in a suspended, yet clear, state. There was only Dawson, the fire keeper and me. The opening round was for chanting to the animal powers, the second – our prayers for the Earth Mother, the third was again the round of the Red Wolf, though with a difference. Dawson had me move to the West door of the lodge. He was at the East door. He took me through a session of deep breathing, using drums and chants to aid me. The journey was to visit my red wolf.

He guided me by trek and canoe to find a stream deep in the mountains. I paddled for a long time until my arms felt very tired. Then turning a bend in the river there was a clearing straight ahead. There stood Wolfie with a female spirit guardian behind him. I beached the canoe and knelt before Wolfie, putting my arms round his strong neck while he licked every part of my face. Then I sat beside him as we looked out at the river. I asked Wolfie,

"Can you tell me why you died when you visited me in Dawson's sweat during the Red Wolf round?"

It was the guardian who softly replied, "This creature so loved you that when he tuned into energies that could harm you in that round of the sweat lodge, he placed himself in their path so you would be spared damage. That is what took his life."

I received this news in silence, placing one hand on Wolfie's back. We just sat side by side watching the flow of the river.

The guardian spoke again, "It is time for you to return."

I took my leave and did not look back at Wolfie, as I could not bear to break down. As I pushed the canoe off the beach into the grip of the river, Wolfie bounded across the clearing and jumped into the canoe.

"He will always be with you in spirit form – protecting you still." As I began to paddle away, I felt the female guardian also step into the canoe. She was coming back with me to provide protection. I did not look back but my heart leapt in joy. I knew she was Trailing Sky Six Feathers from the 18th century. I also knew that she had sent Wolfie to provide me with protection. I paddled away with deep gratitude and happiness, knowing that the energy of Wolfie and Trailing Sky surrounded me. I came back from the journey when Dawson splashed some water on my face. The final round was a thanksgiving round as I was instructed by Dawson to keep Wolfie and Trailing Sky in my mind and heart. The journey was over.

Dawson smiled and I bowed deeply to him. This was the greatest gift he ever gave to me."

The quiet was palpable. No-one talked for a while. We just sat under the branches of the majestic cottonwood as the evening cradled us. Then Sam very softly said,

"I heard this story from one of Dawson's friends, but just thought it was a tall tale his old cronies put out after he was gone." He pursed his lips a bit and then let out a long breath, "I should be paying you for this trip."

I smiled at Sam, re-assuring him that this was not so. Thanks to him, Carolyn and I had learned something very significant for our sacred journey to this region of Arizona. Without his insight to bring us to this ancient medicine wheel, we would not have had such a confirmation or enjoyed a deep sharing between strangers. And for this, Carolyn and I were exceedingly grateful.

"Confirmation is it?" Sam shouted in delight. "You two must be joined at the hip. Whatever your mission is – my every best wish. What the heck am I going to tell the other guides? They will never believe this." Then he grinned mischievously: "But I sure do!"

The very next day Carolyn and I went to Boynton Canyon. Kachina Woman was still there as guardian and reminder. We both said prayers for the Earth Mother before following the trail in to the canyon. It was now quite different to what I remembered. It had been a few years since I had travelled there, twice on my own and once experiencing the cave of the mother with Rion. The experience had intensified every time. During those visits

I had gone alone to Rainbow Bridge with similar intensifying effects. The Boynton Canyon trail was cordoned off with Forestry Service signs to stay on the trail, as the surrounding ecosystem was fragile. I had intended to take Carolyn to the cave of the earth goddess but I could not find the incline from the trail that led to it. Not that we could have taken it, as access to the higher reaches of the canyon was restricted. But the cave was not what I was to find on this journey with Carolyn.

We walked a long way into the box canyon of Boynton. So much of it was new to me. The forest around the entrance changed to shrubs as we eventually came into a grassy clearing where the three arms of the canyon meet. This large open space had the rockface of the canyon on the west side opposite the pinyon forest beyond the shrubs to the east. I noticed the natural shelves of the rockface and the open expanse of the clearing. I paused in the centre of the clearing and as I did so, the hair on the back of my neck felt as though it was being stretched. I was remembering.

I had placed my medicine bundle in my pack before we began this day's journey into Boynton Canyon. I had cedar leaves, sage and tobacco. I carried water in my flask and poured it on the ground in the four directions and to the Earth Mother at the centre - I offered humility and gratitude. Carolyn sat quietly nearby, observing intensely what I was doing. She knew. After the offerings were made I said to her:

"This is the clearing where Trailing Sky and I first met in the 18th century." Although my voice felt as if it came from far away, Carolyn was not surprised.

"Her people from the mountains and mine from the river met for a trading parley. I had traded for two small horses and she for the first time came with her father's expedition. We got here first. Then the mountain people came, having crossed into this canyon from the north. They came in carefully in ones and twos. Then Trailing Sky walked in leading a small pinto horse. I had never seen anyone like her and could not even speak, just handing a bunch of feathers to her as I remained dumb as an ox."

"I thought it was something like that," Carolyn said.

"You know Ian, I think this is a reminder to both of us before we go to meet her on Rainbow Bridge, don't you think so?"

She smiled at me. "It's time to go and enjoy the evening at Quail Ridge. Tomorrow we will travel to Rainbow Bridge"

Our rental car made it through the ruts, gouged out by the heavy rains and we reached the trailhead that led into the rock arch. This is what we had come for, all the way from Canada. Carolyn parked the car where it would benefit from some shade during the afternoon. No other vehicle was there. I remembered the way from my past three visits to Rainbow Bridge. There was no hurry as we walked through this vivid terrain for several miles that had felt so eerie on my first trek there. A great calm and contentment settled over us as we approached the stone arch. Carolyn's response to seeing the arch was similar to mine of many years ago, when I first encountered

Rainbow Bridge. I had not pointed it out to her. Yet, once seeing it she was astonished and knew immediately the power and mystery emanating from it. I placed offerings of sage, tobacco and cedar leaves at the base of the rock arch. We climbed the path leading to the archway and sat down close by to observe and feel it. We felt the wind, the sun, grit of the sandstone and the awesome arch of Rainbow Bridge. Then it was time.

A wind had picked up, so Carolyn and I crawled out to the centre of the stone arch, not looking down. We sat back-to-back – partly for reassurance of safety, but also because this was how we were to sit. After calming our breathing, Carolyn spontaneously began to chant Native American songs that she knew – Seneca, Shoshone and Hopi. As she sang, a beautiful yellow butterfly alighted on the rock at the centre of the arch, right next to her bare feet. It stayed there until she finished chanting – then it flew away. I felt the internal rumble of dimensions opening and felt an enormous charge of energy coming through me. I still felt calm and could detect a distinct female energy traversing the dimensions to settle on the archway with Carolyn and me.

Time passed slowly. I could feel waves of strong energy pulsing from the rock arch and from the sky directly above us. The wind was gusting strongly, enough to ruffle our hair and clothing - but without any sense of danger. The feminine energy settled all around us, invited in by the yellow butterfly at Carolyn's feet. It was utterly overwhelming.

My eyes were half closed as I stayed alert to what was happening around and within us. No-one came near.

There was an uncanny stillness in the trees and canyon beneath us, despite the wind. Later on I sensed the dimensions closing with a grating kind of feeling. I knew the doors were being shut. The feminine energy was still there and I assumed it was attached to Carolyn. I mentioned to Carolyn that it was now time to get off the archway. She crawled off first. I had to turn around and follow her – still not looking down. We sat for a while at the edge. I could recall Rion playing his flute there and gently asked Carolyn whether she could hear it too. She just smiled. We sat there until the onset of sunset – taking it all in with a feeling of great gratitude for the mystery of what had taken place. I had not grasped its full significance, though Carolyn had. She remained silent about her insights.

Next day we were resting in the hot tub by the pool at Quail Ridge. I asked Carolyn if she felt anything different.

She said, "No."

But it was me who felt different. I was totally scrambled, sleeping long hours, feeling very heavy and slow. I had experienced deep visceral sensations while on Rainbow Bridge, but did not understand them. Over breakfast several mornings later Carolyn placed her hand over mine.

"My dear Ian, I believe you did not understand what was happening on Rainbow Bridge." She paused to ensure she had my full attention. "Trailing Sky did not come through to me as you may have anticipated or hoped for. Remember her precise words to you from that other time. She said – "I will find you." And that is who she integrated with on Rainbow Bridge a few days ago. I have noticed these last few nights how still you were as you slept. I know you were absorbing Trailing Sky's energy. I also know this same energy will come through to me from you."

She looked at me with her beautiful green eyes and smiled:

"I am glad you were mistaken Ian, because this is so much bigger than either of us anticipated. It binds us together with a greater strength from the past. I am happy with that – and also with The Deer cards."

Then she laughed at the thought of our mutual selection of The Deer card. I returned her smile and love, relieved by her gentle wisdom and laughter.

As much as I wanted to accept what Carolyn was saying to me, I avoided the full implications of the mystery. Despite the fact that I began to feel Trailing Sky's energy within myself and within Carolyn in ever deepening ways – I resisted what the sacred canyons and Rainbow Bridge brought to me. Despite the fact that I could feel barriers melting inside of me – I still could not fully accept it. The resistance was from my intellect. I desperately held on to all my limitations of logic and mind. This persisted for several months of uneasy indecision and utter restlessness. Until four months later when I experienced a dream vision at Fish Lake in Orlando, Florida.

Return to The Cave

January 26, 2008, was the peak of my training in Remembering, the letting go of resistance to all that Trailing Sky meant to me.

I had placed a large, underlined asterisk in my diary next to the page for Saturday, January 26, 2008. Shera, a trusted and gifted astrologer friend, had repeatedly insisted that this date was mega significant for me. It completed a two hundred and thirty-one year cycle stretching back in time from January 26, 2008 to 1777. I had a healthy skepticism about astrology, yet learned how brilliant a scientist she was, with a mystic's gift of startling insight. Her accuracy was uncanny, detailed and constantly surprising. Her science was rigorous as she used the ancient texts for me, in addition to standard reference material.

What struck Shera very forcibly as she researched my intersecting charts was Pluto peaking in Capricorn in every one of my 2008 astrological charts. She also noted, with some relief, that this signified the end of struggle for me. The internal battles were done, karma reversed, so I could look forward to ease and alignment. This date was the major watershed of my lives.

It so happened that in the week leading up to January 26, 2008, I was at Fish Lake on the west side of Orlando, Florida with Carolyn. My friends and hosts had a beautiful home on the shoreline of this conservation lake at the end of the Butler Lake chain. They invited me to their home each year to offer teachings to the Buddhist community in Orlando. Neither they nor I had any inkling of how significant this particular visit would be for me. There were few houses on the lake and so many wonderful creatures. All I needed was a pair of binoculars and a mug of coffee on their deck for paradise to unfold. The delight of seeing so many animals, birds, otters, possums and occasional alligator was almost unspeakable.

With the approach of the 26th looming up in my diary I had decided to prepare by fasting and meditating deeply. There was actually no choice. I came down with a stomach flu. Nothing that went into my mouth would stay down. Whatever bug had railroaded me. I actually welcomed it, as the fast was definitely on, accompanied by a gentle entry into prolonged meditation that took me into deep humility and gratitude to be in such a rare cradle of nature. But I was not tuning in at all to this two hundred and thirty-one year cycle that my astrology friend Shera had been so emphatic about. No radical insights emerged, just jumbled rubbish dreams. Perhaps a clearing of my junk was taking place due to Pluto crashing into Capricorn with its usual uprooting panache. The only thing I noticed on the evening before January 26th was that my focus suddenly became enlarged, as though my mind had moved from a small TV screen to a huge HD model. A heightened lucidity that I attributed to being ill and light headed from the fasting. During the night I had a vivid dream vision and remembered every exact detail. It was accompanied by a narrator speaking to me, which I found odd.

I was standing on the lip of a cave high in a canyon in the Red Rock country of Central Arizona. An eagle flew up to me and alighted on my back. She wrapped her wings around me. The gentleness of the talons on my back and the embracing wings across my chest showed me that it was a female golden eagle. Her head was above mine, looking out from the cave. I could see through her eyes.

Then the narrator's voice said "This is the protection of the great eagle. Trailing Sky Six Feathers gives it to you."

Then the mountain lion bounded into the cave and I heard a different voice in the dream – Trailing Sky speaking through the eagle. "This is the heart and courage of the mountain lion that I now give to you."

The deer came in, followed by owl and bear – all medicine gifts from Trailing Sky. The wily coyote trotted in – the gift of strategy and discernment.

The narrator spoke again, "This goes on throughout the night as you sleep. The gifts of Trailing Sky Six Feathers given to you. Remember well, she is the greatest medicine woman the South West has ever known. Remember well, she is the direct expression of the highest universal plane. She had only one wish when you died in her arms two hundred and thirty-one years ago – to find you. Receive the gifts she could not give to you before you died. They arose in her to fill the void of your passing from her life. She has been waiting a long time. You promised her the last time you were in the cave sanctuary that you would understand and not resist."

"You now carry Trailing Sky's medicine bundle. Your illness was sent by her, so you would prepare without resistance. She connects to holy beings in all traditions. Guidance from her is not trivial and cannot ever be taken lightly. Your responsibility is to honor this. Your insights into the reality of Trailing Sky will become clear."

When I awoke next morning, I recalled the dream vision in precise detail. Suddenly I had a searing vision of Trailing Sky holding me in her arms as I died in 1777 at the medicine wheel on the rock bluff above the weeping willow tree. I was harrowed to the bone by her grief. I felt her fierceness and anger at the other-worldly beings for failing to revive me. Then felt her anger release as she concentrated on my passage through time and space. I saw how she sat in the medicine wheel holding my dead body as she chanted our journey. I watched her hair turn grey, then white. Then saw her majestic communication to The People. I remember before death, looking up at her and smiling my love through my eyes to her and can still hear her say:

"I will find you my husband, I will find you."

And she did – two hundred and thirty-one years later. I could not at first believe this or fully accept it. Yet the eagle wings around me were her arms, the eagle head above mine – her vision and fierceness, the talons digging gently into my back – to ensure that I understood. In that instant I totally surrendered to this relentless Muse that never gave up on me. I gave up all resistance, realizing that Trailing Sky had kept her word from 1777:

"I will find you."

Even now, as I write this memory down, I cannot stop the tears. I am both here, with the dream vision and there, dying in the medicine wheel, as she vows to find me. All my reservations and doubts become as nothing.

On wakening my wife Carolyn, I related the vision of Trailing Sky Six Feathers in eagle form. That she had offered her medicine gifts. I had finally fully "Remembered." So much from that time was flooding my mind. Carolyn knew about Trailing Sky, the astrological prophecy from Shera and my preparation. I had asked her if she would focus on this cycle of time and space as I would surely miss it, as I felt so out of it. She focused, and dreamed that she was dancing an earth dance. I remembered that too – Trailing Sky had danced that way in the sacred ceremony that bonded us several centuries ago.

My life changed forever after that dream vision took me back to Trailing Sky's prophecy. I recalled to memory her last step across the lip of the cave when she stopped and went into a trance. I remember stepping closer to support her from falling. She had turned and spoke in a voice scarcely her own. "You will return to this cave in dreamtime, though not in this lifetime. Hear me now – understand the vision and do not resist what it teaches. Hear me – and promise me."

I knew that the medicine gifts received from Trailing Sky during the dream vision required that I nurture the skills within me to use them wisely. I entered deeply into silence, meditation and reflection about the dream vision, keeping this all to myself with the exception of Carolyn. From my training in different wisdom traditions, I brought together the power inherent in them into the mental medicine wheel taught to me by White Eagle Woman. This was the altar, the preparation to honour this great being Trailing Sky Six Feathers. In the centre of the medicine wheel mandala our daily conversations began.

Shortly afterwards, Carolyn left Fish Lake in Orlando for home in Ottawa. I stayed to offer two further weeks of teachings. I had to take time and care to place the gifts from Trailing Sky in appropriate vessels for understanding and communication to others.

My remaining time at Fish Lake, surrounded by nature and solitude, provided the uninterrupted space to allow this to deepen, so I could fully integrate the portent of the dream vision. I was very quiet, living very simply in a disciplined and light manner, cultivating the vessels. I also had some unexpected help.

A magnificent osprey – fish eagle – had roosted at the top of the dead tree in front of my bedroom window. He was there every sunrise during this time of fasting and insight. I would go out to the balcony on waking up and he would be right there. Not fishing. Not flying. Just there – staring in my direction. He would stay until noon. On a hunch on the third morning, I walked over to the tall dead tree and found several feathers. On the fourth morning, right after the dream vision, I stepped out on to the balcony and there he was again. He stretched his wings, preened his feathers and let out a high-pitched squawk.

"I guess you are there to make sure I got it about the dream vision and Trailing Sky's prophecy."

Whether he picked my thoughts out of the sky I will never know, but with a resounding high-pitched screech he spread his wings and flew in a huge circle over Fish Lake and then headed west up the chain of lakes.

I got dressed and headed over to the tree where he had perched. There were more feathers. I picked them up and added the feathers to my collection. I had not counted them, but when I did – there were exactly six feathers. I started to laugh and had to sit down on the bed as tears of joy and understanding ran down my face. I got the message, and chuckled at the osprey, who could count.

I was in awe of the dream vision, the medicine gifts, and the narrator. The implications for my life were enormous.

All my reservations and doubts were as nothing compared to the gifts bestowed upon me by Trailing Sky.

I did not take the six feathers home with me. I buried them close to the nesting colony of ospreys. They were a communication, not a keepsake.

I enjoyed the quiet paddle through the lake system and buried the six feathers, bound by grass, at the foot of a tree containing a huge osprey nest.

This was my gratitude.

21. Finding

The internal battles are over

as relentless shadowing by the Muse

brings understanding to overcome the past.

Finding myself as a healer, mentor

and educator

to find the true nature so that

humanity and the world may

be renewed.

I reached for my backpack

and took out a writing pad

with its gold-plated pen

to tell the story by hand written.

131

Finding grace, illumination with

wonder and awe.

The man in the flesh, blood and bones

is the receiver and giver

of love to all crossing my path.

22. **Rooted in my Sovereignty**

The 1X of Pentacles

reflects where I am right now - awake,

serving and grateful.

My narrative goes to extraordinary lengths

to understand.

A learning experience

to stretch beyond myself

by teachers that gave new choices.

I am clear with my directions

at this perfect time and way

- with a strong sense of inner peace

-   and security.

I stretch myself beyond my years

To a full and abundant life.

I see the valve of the

journey I have been on.

Every moment.

PUBLICATIONS - THE AUTHOR'S WORKS

To the best of my ability, I endeavor to follow Gandhi's principles of *ahimsa* (do not harm) and the teachings on mindfulness. These are the guidelines and foundations for my peace and environmental activism.

I live very simply as a planetary activist, Zen teacher, and recognized guru in India. My initial task is to refine my own consciousness - to be a vehicle to chart an authentic path.

The focus on daily mindfulness enables me to be still and clear. My passion for the preservation of Mother Earth propels me to serve the planet and humanity by creating bridges and pathways of mindfulness for community activism. Over the past fifty years I have penned twenty books. My hope is to get your attention!

I have transformed several writings from my prior books to cast a sharper short story more suitable to this collection. I thank respective editors Mark Rossi, Bob Barclay and Michel Weatherall for their belief in my work.

* New Directions in Economic Anthropology. Special Edition of the Canadian Review of Sociology and Anthropology, 1973

*   Reflections: The Anthropological Muse
American Anthropological Association, 1985

*   Leadership and Ethics
RSVK India, May 1997

*   Anthropology at the Edge: Essays on Culture,
Symbol and Consciousness
University Press of America, 1997

*   The Essential Spiral: Ecology and Consciousness
After 9/11
University Press of America, 2002

*   Failsafe: Saving the Earth From Ourselves
Manor House Publishing, 2008

*   Earth My Body, Water My Blood
Baico Publishing Inc, 2011

*   Song of Silence
Baico Publishing Inc, 2011

*   Portals and Passages: Book 1 and Book 2
eBooks on Amazon.com Kindle, 2012

*   Keeping Dharma Alive: Volume 1 and Volume 2
        eBooks on Amazon.com Kindle, 2012

*   Redemption
        Xlibris LLC, 2014

*   Trailing Sky Six Feathers: One Man's Journey
        with His Muse
        Xlibris LLC, 2014

*   New Planet New World
        Manor House Publishing, 2016

*   Painting With Words: Poetry for a New Era
        Manor House Publishing, 2018

*   Shattered Earth: Approaching Extinction
        Manor House Publishing, 2019

*   Past, Present and Future: Stories that Haunt
        Manor House Publishing, 2021

*   Four Phases, Lost, Impermanence, Bittersweet,
        Caring
        Manor House Publishing, 2022

* 2 CD's and 2 DVD's

* 4 films

* 8 Professional Honors, 5 book awards

* 10 Scientific and Technical reports

* 200 professional articles/chapters/book reviews
  published

* 26 Electronic television courses broadcast
  at Carleton University TVO

* 50 articles in Pine Gate – Online Buddhist Journal

Manor House
www.manor-house-publishing.com
905-648-4797

Manor House
www.manor-house-publishing.com
905-648-4797